*S*urprises are
wrapped up
With paper and bow

And hidden in cupboards
Where secrets won't show.

3

Surprises are often
Good things to eat;

A get-well toy or
A birthday *treat*.

CONTENTS

Surprises

A Poem to Share

Written by Jean Conder Soule

Photographed by Mary Foley

Surprises are r⊙und

Or *long* or tallish.

Surprises are SQUARE

Or flat and smallish.

2

Surprises come
In such interesting siZes.

I *like* surprises!

The Birthday Present

Written by Anna Watts
Photographed by Mary Foley

Arista and her big brother, Joe, went to buy Mum a birthday present.

"What shall we buy?" asked Joe.

"I know what Mum likes," said Arista.

Arista took Joe
into a shop.

"What are you buying
here?" asked Joe.

"Film for our camera,"
said Arista.

Arista took Joe
into another shop.

"What are you buying
here?" asked Joe.

"A nice frame
for a photo,"
said Arista.

Arista took Joe
into another shop.

"What are you buying
here?" asked Joe.

"A big yellow bow,
some green wrapping paper,
and a card to write on,"
said Arista.

Arista took Joe
into another shop.
"Stand here, please, Joe,"
she said.

Arista asked the man
in the shop
to take a photo.

"Say cheese!"
said the man.

"This is what Mum likes,"
said Arista. "Us!"

16

Playing Ball

Written by Dawn McMillan
Illustrated by Helen Humphries

Matt and Sarah
and James went to play
in the park.

Sarah hit the ball up
in the air and over into
Mrs McGregor's garden.

Mrs McGregor looked up.
She looked down.
The ball was
under a cabbage.

"Here you are,"
said Mrs McGregor.
She threw the ball
to Matt.

Matt hit the ball
up in the air again.
It went over the fence
and into Mrs McGregor's
tomatoes.

Mrs McGregor looked
for the ball.

"At least this ball
isn't red like
my tomatoes!" she said.
She threw the ball
to James.

James hit the ball.
Away it went
into the garden again!

25

"My beans!"
shouted Mrs McGregor.
"Your game is not good
for my garden.
I will help you
stop the ball.
I will play, too!"

Mrs McGregor took off
her gardening gloves.
She went out of her gate
and played ball, too.

She caught
the high balls.

She dived for
the low balls.

She ran after
the fast balls.

Now Mrs McGregor
plays in the park
every Saturday.

She has new shorts.
She has a new cap.
She runs and jumps.
She catches the ball.

"This is a good way
to keep my garden safe,"
she says. "I like
playing ball!"

The Little Brown House

Written by Joy Cowley
Illustrated by Jo Davies

In the little brown house,
there lived a little woman
and her hen and her cat.

One morning,
the little woman
got up and looked
in her cupboard.
It was empty.

"There is no breakfast!"
said the little woman.
"I might as well
go back to bed."

She got into
her little bed
and pulled the covers
up to her head.

The little brown house
felt sorry for her.
It said, "Whisper, whisper,"
to the fire.

The fire said,
"Crackle, crackle,"
to the kettle.

The kettle said,
"Bubble, bubble,"
to the clock.

The clock said,
"Tick-tock, tick-tock,"
to the cat.

The cat said,
"Meow, meow,"
to the hen.

The hen said,
"Cluck-cluck, cluck-cluck,"
and laid a little
brown egg.

The cat put the egg
in the kettle
and put the kettle
over the fire.

"Crackle, crackle,"
said the fire
to the kettle.

"Bubble, bubble,"
said the kettle
to the clock.

"Tick-tock, tick-tock,"
said the clock
to the cat.

"Meow, meow,"
said the cat.

She took the egg
out of the kettle
and put it in an eggcup.

Then the cat and the hen
went to the little woman.

"Breakfast!" they said.

The little woman
sat up in bed.
"Thank you, Hen!
Thank you, Cat, Clock,
Kettle, and Fire!
And thank you,
Little Brown House!"

The hen smiled
at the cat.
The cat smiled
at the clock.
The clock smiled
at the kettle.
The kettle smiled
at the fire.

The fire smiled
at the little brown house.
The little brown house
smiled to itself,
as it said, "Whisper,
whisper, whisper."